BODY LANGUAGE

Workbook for Nonverbal Communication

JOHN J. TROMBETTA, PH.D.

outskirts
press

Body Language
Workbook for Nonverbal Communication
All Rights Reserved.
Copyright © 2022 John J. Trombetta, Ph.D.
v2.0

Outskirts Press, Inc.
http://www.outskirtspress.com

ISBN: 978-1-9772-4920-3

Outskirts Press and the "OP" logo are trademarks belonging to Outskirts Press, Inc.

PRINTED IN THE UNITED STATES OF AMERICA

*In memory of
my father, Nicholas
my mother, Anna
and
my sister, Jean*

Acknowledgments

To my wife, Joanna, son, Justin, and sister,
Linda who through their support and
encouragement made the creation
of this work possible.

And, to my daughter Jessica, son-in-law Ryan,
grandson Jackson and granddaughter
Grace for their love.

Table of Contents

Preface

If you are ever going to work with people, then this workbook in nonverbal communication will be useful. Almost without exception books on nonverbal communication state that an individual is constantly sending some message, either consciously or unconsciously. But more importantly, research has shown that when the verbal message is in conflict with the nonverbal message, people believe the nonverbal cue. For these reasons, knowledge of nonverbal communication will make you a more effective communicator—an asset in any career.

Nonverbal communication is not as rigidly structured as other communications; nevertheless, our society does impose some rules on nonverbal behavior.

The exercises in this workbook will increase your awareness of the rules of nonverbal behavior and will also increase your ability to understand, control, and interpret nonverbal cues.

Researchers have identified more than five thousand hand signals that people use in normal conversation. It is not the individual gesture, facial expression, or tone of voice that you will need to learn but rather the complete picture. The activities that precede a particular gesture are just as relevant as the gesture itself. A smile is not always a sign of happiness, any more than crossed arms are always a sign of rejection.

This workbook has been divided into chapters with the following three categories of exercises for each chapter:

CAN WE TALK? is devoted to discussion questions that will stimulate your thinking.

ACTIONS SPEAK LOUDER THAN WORDS is a section of in-class exercises to increase your "feel" for nonverbal behavior.

ON YOUR OWN TIME is a section of exercises and research projects that will increase your understanding of nonverbal behavior by using your own power of observation.

UNIT 1
INTRODUCTION TO NONVERBAL COMMUNICATION

Can We Talk?

Objectives To explore the relationship between nonverbal communication and verbal communication and become more aware of nonverbal communication in everyday life.

A. Is there an interdependence between verbal and nonverbal stimuli?

    1. Based on your answer, explain how interdependence or lack of interdependence affects the way we study nonverbal communication.

B. It has been noted that one of the most rejecting insults that one individual can use against another is to refuse to shake an outstretched hand. Why do you agree or disagree with this statement?

C. Imagine that you have entered a room occupied with several of your friends and they all stop talking the moment they see you. What do you think about their behavior? How do you feel? What other conclusions could you have drawn? Share your thoughts with the class and relate any real-life instances where you have made snap judgments based on inadequate information.

D. How are the following terms concerned with the study of nonverbal communication: *kinesics, proxemics, paralanguage, tactile,* and *olfactory*.

E. It has been stated that an individual is more likely to believe your nonverbal communication than the words you say. From your experience, do you agree or disagree? Be prepared to defend your position.

Actions Speak Louder Than Words

Objective: To enable students to gauge the success of their nonverbal communication skills

A. A student from the class should volunteer for the following exercise:

Standing in front of the class, the student should attempt to convey five of the following emotions using only nonverbal(non-vocal) body and facial communication. Members of the class will attempt to guess the correct emotion.

thoughtful	tense	jealous
shy	suspicious	cautious
confident	sad	domineering
angry	happy	anxious
nervous	confused	awkward

The class should now discuss how these emotions were primarily conveyed.

Objective: To help the student realize how much nonverbal communication plays a role in the acquaintance process

B. Each student should select a member of the class whom he/she has not previously met. After a five-minute "getting to know you" conversation, each student should note the amount of meaning that was conveyed through verbal versus nonverbal communication. For instance, 75 percent of the conversation was conveyed through nonverbal cues and 25 percent through verbal communication. Also note the types of nonverbal communication (hand gestures, facial expressions, body position) utilized during the conversation. The instructor should initiate a class discussion concerning this exercise.

Objective: To make the student aware of nonverbal factors that influence perceptions

C. During the first or second meeting of the class, try this exercise. Students are requested to find a partner who is a stranger and sit together without speaking. Each of the partners will fill out Form A based on visual observation, intuition, and assumption. About ten minutes is sufficient for this task. Upon completion of Form A*, each participant fills out another Form A about himself/herself. In this case, without verbal communication, individuals try to guess what their partners have written about them. Do not necessarily use actual facts about age, marital status, etc., but rather simply guess what, through appearance and nonverbal cues, someone else may be assuming about you. Forms may be exchanged and shared.

*Form A is on the next two pages.

Nonverbal Exercise - Form A

1. Silently complete this form answering the question strictly by your observation of your partner. Do not attempt to signal nonverbal answers deliberately in any way.

2. Silently complete another Form A about yourself, estimating what you suppose your partner has written about you (not the actual facts about yourself).

3. When both forms have been completed by both partners, you may speak. Discuss and review the forms or just exchange.

4. Check one: This sheet to be used for
   ___ Nonverbal observation of partner
   ___ Nonverbal estimate of partner's observation of you

   Willingness to participate sincerely in this exercise

   Degree of anxiety about participating in this exercise

   Estimated age: _______ **Place of birth:_________ Month of birth:________**

   Marital status:
   Married ____ Single ____ Divorced ____ Separated ____ Widowed ____

   Estimated maximum education: __________

   Nationality: ___________________

   Occupation: 1st guess __________________ 2nd guess___________________

Interests:

_____ dancing	_____ gourmet foods and drinks
_____ spectator sports	_____ artistic and creative, type
_____ participant sports	_____ TV
_____ music, type	_____ writing
_____ movies, type	_____ camping, hiking
_____ reading, type	_____ travel
_____ participating in membership organizations	_____ politics
	_____ sewing, cooking

COMMENTS

Religious belief:

First guess____

Second guess______________________________________

Practice:

strong _____   moderate _____   little _____   none _____

NONVERBAL EXERCISE - FORM A

1. Silently complete this form answering the question strictly by your observation of your partner. Do not attempt to signal nonverbal answers deliberately in any way.

2. Silently complete another Form A about yourself, estimating what you suppose your partner has written about you (not the actual facts about yourself).

3. When both forms have been completed by both partners, you may speak. Discuss and review the forms or just exchange.

4. Check one: This sheet to be used for
___ Nonverbal observation of partner
___ Nonverbal estimate of partner's observation of you

Willingness to participate sincerely in this exercise
Degree of anxiety about participating in this exercise

Estimated age: _______ **Place of birth**:_________ **Month of birth**:________

Marital status:
Married _____ Single _____ Divorced _____ Separated _____ Widowed _____

Estimated Maximum education__________

Nationality: ___________________

Occupation: 1st guess __________________   2nd guess__________________

Interests:

_____ dancing	_____ gourmet foods and drinks
_____ spectator sports	_____ artistic and creative, type
_____ participant sports	_____ TV
_____ music, type	_____ writing
_____ movies, type	_____ camping, hiking
_____ reading, type	_____ travel
_____ participating in membership organizations	_____ politics
	_____ sewing, cooking

COMMENTS

Religious belief:

First guess____

Second guess____

Practice:
strong _______ moderate _______ little _______ none _______

	None	Little	Moderate	Much
Flexibility				
Receptivity to change				
Degree of personal warmth				
Degree of openness about self				
Generosity				
Self-confidence				
Sense of humor				
Ability to receive				
Concern for others				
Openness to consider new ideas				
Ease of establishing friendships				

leader	follower	impatient	insightful
aggressive	assertive	rigid	extrovert
passive	patient	shy	introvert*

Reference:
   Leonard Zunin, *Contact The First Four Minutes*, (New York: Ballantine Books) pp. 255-258. Copyright (c) 1975. Reprinted by permission of Nash Publishing Corp.

On Your Own Time

Objective: To allow the student to become aware of the importance that nonverbal skills play in the communication process

    A. Plan to attend an on-campus guest presentation or class lecture. Choose a speaker who is known for his/her outstanding speaking ability. Following the presentation or lecture prepare a report that examines the speaker's vocal communication (voice rate, pitch, volume, and vocal variety) and nonverbal communication (eye contact, facial expressions, hand gestures, body position, personal appearance, etc.)

Objective: To illustrate the functions of nonverbal communication in the communication process

    B. Form groups of eight to twelve people. Through some random procedure, each group is divided into two sections or subgroups. The entire group should watch the same half-hour television show, to be selected by the entire group, for example situational comedies or dramas where you have familiarity with the characters, but not with the plot. Soap operas would be inappropriate, since you would have to know too much about the plot to analyze it. One-half of the group (the A's) should watch the show without any sound; the other half (the B's) should watch the show with sound. After viewing the show, the entire group should get together. The students who viewed the show without sound should attempt to summarize the plot. The B's should not interrupt or correct the A's while they are attempting to reconstruct the plot. This non-intervention will be most difficult, but it is essential. After the attempted summary or reconstruction of the plot by the group who viewed the show without sound, the other half of the group who viewed the show with sound should attempt to specify the ways in which the reconstruction was inaccurate and the possible reasons for it. After the basic plot has been accurately summarized by the B's, this time assisted by the A's, the entire group should consider some or all of the following issues:

1. What gross bodily movements are used to communicate?

2. What messages did facial expressions communicate?

3. What did the eyes communicate?

4. How were hand gestures used, and what did they communicate?

5. What messages did clothes and general appearance communicate?

6. How was space used to communicate? What messages did it communicate?

7. Was touch used to communicate? What messages did it communicate?

8. What conclusions do you draw concerning the relative contribution of sound and bodily movements in communication? *

*Reference:
Pp. 334-335, 6.3 Nonverbal Communication from *The Elements of Public Speaking* 2nd edition by Joseph A. DeVito. Copyright (c) 1984 by Joseph A. DeVito. Reprinted by permission of Harper & Row, Publishers Inc.

UNIT 2
PHYSICAL APPEARANCE AND DRESS

Can We Talk?

A. How are people's status and vocation expressed by the clothing they wear? Do you agree that one must dress successfully to be successful? Describe the type of clothing that a high-ranking corporate head would wear. Name some organizations that clothing is used to identify one's rank. Are corporate dress codes as well defined for women as they are for men?

B. In our day-to-day living there are people who receive only minimal attention, for example beggars. Is there a relationship between our lack of attention to them and the way they are dressed? Are there other people or groups of people who receive little attention because of their clothing choices?

C. Silent movies relied heavily on clothing and exaggerated gestures to identify the villain and hero. Are these same techniques used in today's films? Give examples that support your answer.

D. Have you ever had to wear a uniform as part of a school or athletic team, for the military, or as a member of a drama performance? Explain how the uniform may have influenced your gestures, posture, and other nonverbal communication behaviors.

E. Body Types

   Fill in each of the blanks below with a word from the list following each statement. A word that exactly describes you may not be in the list, but select the word that seems to describe you most closely. Upon completion of this task go on to answer question six.

I feel _____________, _____________, and _____________most of the time.

calm	relaxed	complacent
anxious	confident	reticent
cheerful	tense	energetic
contented	impetuous	self-conscious

When I study or work, I seem to be_____________, _____________, and _____________.

efficient	placid	leisurely	determined
enthusiastic	sluggish	meticulous	thoughtful
reflective	competitive	precise	cooperative

Socially I am _____________, _____________ and, _____________.

outgoing	gentle-tempered	affected	shy
affable	considerate	soft-tempered	talkative
tolerant	awkward	argumentative	hot-tempered

I am rather _____________, _____________, and _____________.

active	introspective	suspicious	serious
warm	forgiving	cool	soft-hearted
domineering	courageous	sympathetic	enterprising

Other people consider me rather_______________ and _______________.

generous	dominant	reckless	kind
adventurous	optimistic	detached	cautious
withdrawn	affectionate	sensitive	dependent

Underline the one word out of the three in each of the following lines that most closely describes the way you are:

    a. assertive, relaxed, tense
    b. hot-tempered, cool, warm
    c. withdrawn, sociable, active
    d. confident, tactful, kind
    e. dependent, dominant, detached
    f. enterprising, affable, anxious

DO NOT read any farther until you have completed all six questions. The assumption of this test is that people of a particular body type behave in a certain way, a way that is significantly different from the ways people with other body types behave. Three major body types are distinguished: endomorphy, or heavy and generally short; mesomorphy, or muscular; and ectomorphy, or skinny and generally tall. The scoring for this test is done as follows: Match each word that you selected on the test with its corresponding body type as indicated in the list on the next page. The heading on the list from which the greatest number of words were chosen should indicate the body type of the person who chose them. The tendency toward the other two body types should also be indicated by the number of terms selected from each of the other two lists.

ENDOMORPHY	MESOMORPHY	ECTOMORPHY
affable	active	anxious
affected	adventurous	awkward
affectionate	argumentative	cautious
calm	assertive	considerate
complacent	cheerful	cool
contended	competitive	detached

cooperative	confident	gentle-tempered
dependent	courageous	introspective
forgiving	determined	meticulous
generous	dominant	precise
kind	domineering	reflective
leisurely	efficient	reticent
placid	energetic	self-conscious
relaxed	enterprising	sensitive
sluggish	enthusiastic	serious
sociable	hot-tempered	shy
softhearted	impetuous	suspicious
soft-tempered	optimistic	tactful
sympathetic	outgoing	tense
tolerant	reckless	thoughtful
warm	talkative	withdrawn

Note Carefully

The research on which this test is based has been criticized from a number of different points of view. The purpose of this exercise is not to illustrate that these body types are associated with the various personality characteristics (in very many instances they are not), but rather to demonstrate that we seem to expect people of certain body types to be associated with certain personality characteristics. We seem to expect the thin person to be tense, the fat person to be jolly, and the muscular person to be assertive. Often we are wrong, yet we do have various expectations. The major purpose of this exercise is to provide an opportunity for examining our expectations. It should be added that this test has been based on results obtained largely from heterosexual males. The relationships between body type and personality characteristics for women and for homosexual males may be very different from those postulated here. *

Actions Speak Louder Than Words

Objective: To examine the type of clothing used in TV news broadcasting

    A. Tune into the three television networks (ABC, NBC, CBS) to watch the evening newscasts. Compare and contrast the dress of each anchorperson. Are there any impressions all three are attempting to reflect to the audience?

Objective: To illustrate the relationship between dress and general behavior

    B. Go to a restaurant that caters to a varied clientele. Observe how the table servers react to the customers. Do they treat people differently? Is it related to the customer's style of dress? Describe the differences you have experienced upon entering a store in jeans and a sweatshirt as opposed to formal dress.

    C. Complete the following case study or create your own field observation project after consulting with your instructor.

Objective: To help students understand the effects of attire on one's conformity behavior

Research Problem:

What are the behavioral conformity effects of one subject's attire on another at a pedestrian street Wait signal?

    1. Will subjects violate or conform to the restriction (the Wait signal) when a person in high-status attire violates the restriction?

    2. Will subjects violate or conform to the restriction when a person in high-status dress conforms to the restriction?

3. Will subjects violate or conform to the restriction when a person in low-status dress violates the restriction?

4. Will subjects violate or conform to the restriction when a person in low-status dress conforms to the restriction?

Materials and subjects:

1. Individual to serve as high-status model wearing a freshly pressed suit, shined shoes, white shirt, and tie.

2. Individual to serve as low-status model wearing soiled pants, well-worn scuffed shoes, and a wrinkled shirt.

Procedures:

1. Select a location where a pedestrian traffic signal regulates the flow of pedestrians by alternately flashing from Wait to Walk.

2. Determine at what hours the selected location is relatively busy with pedestrians and plan to conduct the experiment during these hours.

3. On the first day the experiment is conducted, use the following order for the presentation of the different treatments:

    model dressed in high-status attire conforms to the Wait signal; that is, she or he crosses the street when the Wait signal changes to Walk for five changes of the lights

    model dressed in low-status attire violates the Wait signal; that is, he or she crosses the street at approximately the midpoint of the Wait interval for five changes of the lights

    model dressed in high-status attire violates the Wait signal in the same manner as described above

    model dressed in low-status attire conforms to the Wait signal in the same manner as described for the model in high-status attire.

Rules for Observing:

1. Only subjects standing with the model before he or she crosses the street are to be included in the data.

2. Only pedestrians reaching at least the middle of the street while the Wait signal flashes are to be considered violating the prohibition.

3. All subjects meeting the first rule of observing, but not the second, are to be considered conforming with the prohibition.

Procedures continuing:

1. After each of the five trials for each treatment condition, record on the data sheet the number of pedestrians who conformed and the number who violated the Wait signal.

2. While the model is absent from the scene, observe the number of pedestrians who violate and conform to the Wait signal, and record these observations on the data sheet. Do this for five changes of the lights.

3. On the second day the experiment is conducted, reverse the order of the treatment conditions used on the first day.

4. Repeat number four.

5. Repeat number five.

What conclusions from this experiment can be drawn about the effects of attire on conformity behavior? Use the answer data sheet form on the next pages.

D. Do most people have an image of a leader?
Cut out three pictures from a newspaper/magazine of individuals in the news. Paste each picture onto the form on the next page, one picture per candidate. Interview at least ten people concerning the question on the next page. Record the interviewee's responses. Discuss the results of your study with the class.

CANDIDATE A	CANDIDATE B	CANDIDATE C

If these three candidates were running for the office of mayor of your town, which one would you vote for based on their appearance?

Data Sheet

Group	*High Status* Model Violates		Model Conforms		*Low Status* Model Absent		Model Violates		Model Conforms	
	Pedes-trian Violates 1	Pedes-trian Conforms 2	Pedes-trian Violates 3	Pedes-trian Conforms 4	Pedes-trian Violates 5	Pedes-trian Conforms 6	Pedes-trian Violates 7	Pedes-trian Conforms 8	Pedes-trian Violates 9	Pedes-trian Conforms 10
Day 1										
Trial 1										
Trial 2										
Trial 3										
Trial 4										
Trial 5										
TOTAL										
Day 2										
Trial 1										
Trial 2										
Trial 3										
Trial 4										
Trial 5										
TOTAL										
*GRAND TOTAL										
**Percent										

* Grand Total = Total (Day 1) + Total (Day 2)

* * To determine the percentages for groups 1 and 2, sum the grand totals for both groups and then divide the sum into each one of the grand totals. Finally, multiply the results by ten to obtain the percentages. Repeat this for the pairs of groups 3 and 4, groups 5 and 6, groups 7 and 8, and groups 9 and 10.

ANSWER SHEET - EFFECTS OF ATTIRE ON CONFORMITY BEHAVIOR

Analyze and compare the results of the data obtained for the four conditions outlined under the research problem.

1. When an individual in high-status violates a pedestrian Wait signal, are others more likely to violate or conform to the same signal? To determine this information, compare percentages recorded on the data sheet.

2. When an individual in high-status attire conforms to a pedestrian Wait signal, are others more likely to violate or conform to the same signal? To determine this information, compare appropriate percentages recorded on the data sheet.

3. When an individual in low-status attire violates a pedestrian Wait signal, are others more likely to violate or conform to the same signal? To determine this information, compare appropriate percentages recorded on the data sheet.

4. When an individual in low-status attire conforms to a pedestrian Wait signal, are others more likely to violate or conform to the same signal? To determine this information, compare percentages recorded on the data sheet.

5. What conclusions can be drawn from the experiment about the effects of attire on conformity behavior? *

*Reference:

Lawrence B. Rosenfeld, Gerald Goldhaber, Val R. Smith, *Experiments in Human Communication* (University of North Carolina, Chapel Hill, North Carolina: Rosenfeld) pp. 178-184. Copyright (c) 1975.Reprinted by permission.

On Your Own Time

Objective: To demonstrate the effect that artifacts and clothing have on our appearance

A. Bring items to class that will help you modify your appearance. Jewelry, makeup, a wig, clothing, etc., would be appropriate articles. Be prepared to demonstrate how these items change your appearance.

Objective: To investigate cultural perceptions of beauty

B. Is there a consensus among female students as to what parts of a male's body are most important in judging attractiveness?
Does this consensus exist among male students in regard to the bodies of females?

To answer these questions, each student in the class should write down on a piece of paper two parts of a male's body (if a female is responding) or a female's body (if a male is responding) that you believe are the most important in judging attractiveness of an individual of the opposite gender. The results should be tallied and placed on the blackboard.

Are you surprised at the results? Why or why not? Do you think that the results reached in this class would be the same results if this survey were conducted among students in another country? In your opinion does a society's perception of attractiveness change with the passage of time? If yes, give several examples.

Objective: To explore the types of clothing used in various career

C. The class should form groups of five people. Using the form on the page below, two groups (call them group A and group B; should agree to work separately on designing the clothes for agreed-upon occupations (for example, a CBS executive, female librarian in a public library, and coal miner). Upon completion of the assignment by both groups, group A and group B should discuss in what ways their dressing of individuals in these occupations were similar or dissimilar. Why were they similar or dissimilar?

EXERCISE: DESIGN CLOTHES FOR ALL OCCUPATIONS

Group_____________________________   Assignment_________________

Directions: Describe the types of clothing (and accessories, if any) worn in each occupation.

1. CBS executive

2. Female librarian in a public library

3. Coal miner

4. Commercial airline pilot

5. Attorney

6. Cowboy

7. University professor

8. Manager at Macy's

9. Firefighter

10. Nurse

11. Farmer

12. Truck driver

13. Football coach

14. Medical doctor

15. Politician

UNIT 3
KINESICS/BODY MOVEMENTS AND GESTURES

Can We Talk?

A. Some researchers of nonverbal communication state that there are universal gestures understood by people in all countries of the world. Other nonverbal communication researchers argue that there are no universal gestures understood worldwide. Do you believe that one of the above groups of researchers is correct? Take a position, and in a class discussion attempt to argue your position using examples, if possible.

Do you believe that in this country there are standard gestures understood by all people? Try this non-scientific exercise in an attempt to answer this question. Two or three students should be chosen to demonstrate three gestures they believe will be correctly interpreted by all the students in the class. After the exercise, the class should engage in a discussion concerning the following questions: Were all the body gestures correctly interpreted by the class? If not, why were these gestures difficult to interpret while the others were easy?

B. What body movements signal to a decoder (receiver) deception, liking and disliking, dominance and submission. Are these movements affected by the decoder's age, education, gender, psychological state, co-culture (French, German, etc. ancestry). Do situational variables affect these bodily movements?

C. Discuss the gestures that people use to describe things, point to things, conciliate others, reject ideas, explain the workings of a machine, and express a willingness to allow another to speak. Are there gestures that allow the receiver of a message to fully understand the emotional state of a sender? Describe some with which you are familiar.

D. By imitating or mirroring a sender's gestures and body movements, a receiver is usually expressing agreement, sympathy, or empathy. Why do you agree or disagree with this statement? If you were attempting to persuade a listener, would

"

you mirror or not mirror the listener's gestures and body movements? Defend your statement.

E. Directions: next to each picture place the attitude which you feel is being portrayed through body posture. In addition, state why you have reached this conclusion. In a class discussion compare your conclusions with others. (Posing: J. Trombetta and C. Vaccaro; Photos by S. Sartori).

1.	
2.	
3.	
4.	
5.	

Actions Speak Louder Than Words

Objective: To help identify which parts of the body communicate emotions best

    A. Do certain parts of the body convey specific emotions more than other parts?

Many researchers of nonverbal communication respond "yes" to this question. To verify this conclusion, each student in the class should individually choose an emotion and the part of the body that they believe best transmits the emotion.

After recording this information on a slip of paper, each student should exchange their slip of paper with another student who, using the part of the body indicated on the slip of paper, will attempt to express the emotion to a small group (three to five students). The small group of students should try to guess what emotion was being expressed.

Objective: To encourage awareness of body movements and gestures as a communication function

    B. Plan a one- to two-minute pantomime in which you use body movements and gestures to prompt an empathic reaction from the class (for instance running and exhaustion or eating and choking, etc.).

Objective: To stimulate kinesics awareness

    c. Using body movements and hand gestures demonstrate a process used in our everyday living (for example sewing, driving a car, cooking a meal, making a sandwich, etc.).

Objective: To illustrate the difficulty or ease of giving nonverbal instructions

D. Have you ever tried to give a set of instructions nonverbally? Here is an exercise that the class can play to explore the difficulty or ease of giving nonverbal instructions.

The class is divided into groups of five or six. One member from each group leaves the room for approximately one minute. When these subjects are out of the room, the instructor gives each group a set of instructions that they must nonverbally communicate to the subject.

In addition the instructor explains the nonverbal cues to which the group is restricted. All groups are given the same instructions.

The first group to get the subject to comply with their instructions wins the round and gets ten points.

The process is repeated with another subject chosen from the group and the instructor issuing the group a different set of instructions and nonverbal cues.

One group will be declared the winner after a certain time is reached or when an agreed-upon point count is reached.

Sample instructions: leave the room, open the window, clap your hands, sit on the floor, comb your hair, etc.

Restricted nonverbal cues: hand and arm movements only, head movements only, tactile cues only, leg movements only, etc.*

*Reference:
Pp. 205-206, 13.1 Instructing Nonverbally from *Communicology: An Introduction to the Study of Communication,* 2nd edition by Joseph A. DeVito. Copyright (c) 1982 by Joseph DeVito. Reprinted by permission of Harper & Row, Publishers Inc.

Objective: To stimulate nonverbal self-awareness

E. MOVEMENT PROFILE

Directions: Answer the following questions as honestly as you can.

1. Upon crossing your legs, which leg is usually on top of the other?

2. On which side of the mouth do you usually do most of your chewing?

3. When you get up to move, which leg is thrust forward first?

4. When you gesture, what is your preferred hand or arm?

5. When you preen, which part of the body gets your primary attention?

6. When you groom your hair, do you use one or both hands? Which hand smooths your hair? Which hand holds a comb or brush?

7. When standing are you conscious of which side of the body you may be leaning or balanced on?

8. When you move your head to say "no," to which direction do you move first?

9. When you yawn, what hand covers your mouth?

10. Is your movement similar to another member of your family? Specify.*

*Reference:
Enid J. Portnoy, Virginia P. Richmond, *Nonverbal Communication Awareness*, (Morgantown, w. Va.: The Book Exchange) p. 39. Copyright (c) undated. Reprinted by permission.

Objective: To identify status and expressiveness conveyed through body position

E. In the drawing below six people are shown in various positions. Rank all participants (L, M, N, X, Y, Z) for the following variables:

Subordinate	Superordinate
Haughty	Humble
Initiating action	Receiving action
Expressive	Inexpressive
Important	Insignificant

Compare your answers with the rest of the class. *

*Reference:

Reprinted with permission of The Free Press, a Division of Macmillan Inc. from *Messages of the Body* by John P. Spiegal and Pavel Machotka. Copyright (c) 1974 by The Free Press

On Your Own Time

Objective: To note the gesture used in two forms of communication

    A. Observe a dyadic (two-person) conversation and then in a public-speaking situation (lectures are acceptable).

    Note any gestures, such as illustrators, affect displays, regulators, and adaptors (look these terms up if not understood) used in the dyadic conversation and then in the public-speaking situation. Are there an equal number of gestures exhibited in both forms of communication? Why or why not? Describe some of the gestures that you noted in one form of communication but not in the other.

Objective: To stimulate awareness of gestures and body movement in various occupations

    B. Some occupations rely heavily on nonverbal communication behavior to perform their tasks. Which occupations can you identify that fit into this category? Which occupations depend totally on gestures and body movement to perform their work? What jobs make no use of gestures and body movement in performing their day-to-day functions?

Objective: To study the communicative role that recording devices play on our body movements and gestures in everyday life

    C. In a paragraph or two explain how monitoring devices such as store cameras might affect your body movements and gestures, such as keeping your hands out of your pockets when exiting a store.

Objective: To determine how culture influences our communicative gestures

    D. According to some researchers, children by the age of one have developed pointing as a communicating gesture. Observe adults and children in teaching communication situations. Does the child or adult point more? Does age seem to affect the use of pointing? Why/why not? If adults use less pointing in communication, what gesture is being used as a substitute for pointing?

Objective: To encourage awareness of ethnic hand gestures and body movements

    E. Are there hand gestures and body movements unique to various ethnic groups? Choose one ethnic group with which you are familiar and describe in a written or spoken paragraph or two that group's particular hand gestures and body moves.

UNIT 4
KINESICS: THE FACE/OCULESICS - FACIAL EXPRESSIONS & EYE BEHAVIOR

Can We Talk

A. Determining Facial Expression

Directions: Bring in six pictures or photos of people displaying the six major facial emotions below. From the neck down cover the bodies of the people in the photos with a sheet of paper and exchange the pictures with a classmate. Have your classmate identify the facial emotions displayed in each picture. Then remove the sheet of paper covering the bodies of the people in the photos and examine the photos again. After determining the emotions expressed by the faces you should look at the rest of the picture to see if there are any conflicts between the facial expressions and the total body. The six primary facial emotions are as follows:

surprise   disgust   fear   happiness   anger   sadness

How accurately did you read the facial expressions of the people in the photos when their bodies were covered from the neck down as opposed to uncovered? If there is a difference between the covered-body photos versus the uncovered body photos, how can this be explained? *

B. Can facial expressions and eye behavior be used to contradict a verbal message, substitute for a verbal message, complement a verbal message, accentuate a verbal message, and regulate a verbal behavior? Explain how this is done.

C. Explain the statement that "The eyes are the windows to the soul." What about the expressions: Spanish eyes, bedroom eyes, the evil eye, in the public eye, keep an eye on it? Can you think of any other expressions that make references to the eye?

D. Do you think there are differences between male and female facial expressions and eye behavior? Defend your position by giving specific instances. Also, are there cultural differences between societies in the use of facial expressions and eye behavior? Finally, do facial expressions and eye behavior change with the age of a person?

*Reference:

Enid J. Portnoy, Virginia Richmond, *Nonverbal Communication Awareness,* (Morgantown, W. Va.: The Book Exchange) p. 47. Copyright (c) undated. Reprinted by permission.

Actions Speak Louder Than Words

Objective: To explore relationship between facial/eye behavior and deception

A. Each student should choose one person in the class with whom to work. Having chosen a partner, the students should place their chairs or desks back to back so they are unable to see the face and eyes of their partner. Reading from the list of statements below, each student should intentionally attempt to deceive their partner by providing incorrect answers to four of the eight statements. After each student completes this part of the exercise, the desks should be placed so that each partner can observe the other's facial and eye expression. The same statements should be read again in the same manner as previously performed. Upon completion of the exercise, each student should inform the other of the true and false responses to the statements.

How many of the statements did you guess correctly when there was no facial and eye observation? How many with facial and eye contact?

Did you change any of your answers because of observing the facial expression and eye behavior of your partner? Can you make any observations concerning deception between people on the telephone or in a cross-examination during a trial in a courtroom?

Statements	Answers	
	Back to Back	**Face to Face**
1. My favorite food is _________	T or F	T or F
2. My favorite subject _________	T or F	T or F
3. My favorite type of music is _________	T or F	T or F
4. Briefly describe what you would like to be doing career-wise five years from now _________	T or F	T or F
5. Briefly describe the members of your family _________	T or F	T or F
6. Briefly describe a frightening experience _________	T or F	T or F
7. Briefly describe a pleasant experience _________	T or F	T or F
8. How many credits have you completed so far toward your degree?	T or F	T or F

Objective: To investigate if facial expressions and eye behavior reflect like or dislike

B. Each member of the class should bring in pictures of three different items to class. At least one item should be pleasing to look at. (Example: an expensive ring, a puppy, etc.) Exchange pictures in class. Before viewing what pictures they have received, students should go to the front of the class and look at the pictures individually. The class must decide from the facial expressions and eye behavior which picture was *most pleasing* to the student. (Note: The class should pay strict attention to any slight movement of the facial muscles and eye movement of their classmate viewing the pictures, which might offer clues.)

Objective: To identify any differences of eye movements between males and females

C. Try this mini-research exercise. You will need two males and two females for this mini-research. Position yourself directly opposite the person to observe their lateral eye movements (LEM). Ask eight simple questions about their background (for example where were you born, how many sisters do you have, etc.). Instruct them to answer four questions truthfully and four as a lie. Note the gender of each respondent on your chart as you record on the chart below their (LEM) lateral eye movement— for example left (L) or right (R)—as they answer each question. Analyze the results on the chart and discuss any differences between the male and female subjects' eye movements when they answered truthfully and when they lied.*

Subject	Q1	Q2	Q3	Q4	Q5	Q6	Q7	Q8

*Reference:

Enid J. Portnoy, Virginia P. Richmond, *Nonverbal Communication Awareness,* (Morgantown, W. Va.: The Book Exchange) p. 58. Copyright (c) undated. Reprinted by permission

Objective: To prove that facial cues speak louder than words

D. Directions: Next to each picture place the emotion being expressed and the facial cues that enabled you to reach your conclusion. In a class discussion, compare your answers with other students.

A.

____
____
____
____
____
____

B.

____
____
____
____
____
____

C.

____
____
____
____
____
____

D.

____
____
____
____
____
____

E.

F.

G.

H.

Posing: John Trombetta
Photos by: Stephen Sartori
Photo Editing: Amrita Stuetzle

On Your Own Time

Objective: To clarify the uses of facial expressions

    A. Is a smile a social response or an emotional response? For one week record examples of people you encounter from other countries when smiling was used to express an emotion (for example happy, sad) and examples when it was used as a social gesture (for example greeting someone). Was the non-native person's use of facial expressions the same as that of a native of this country? Share your findings with other researchers.

Objective: To report on the importance of eye contact in communication

    B. During three separate meals, carry on a conversation with family or friends deliberately avoiding eye contact. Report your results to the class. Include the reactions and comments made by others during this exercise. How did you feel while doing this exercise? Did your eye behavior interrupt the flow of conversation? How?

Objective: To observe the portrayal of facial and eye behavior in art/history photographs

    C. Take a tour of the college or community art gallery (or look through art history books that contain photographs) to find pictures/sculptures that show facial and eye expressions. Did the date when the artwork was completed influence the facial and eye expressions used in the photographs? How? Does the nationality of the artist influence the facial and eye expressions used in the work? What other factors might have influenced the facial and eye expressions portrayed in the art piece?

Objective: To study eye movements that regulate conversation

> D. Observe two different ongoing conversations between three or four persons. Note at least two different eye movements that help regulate the communication interaction.

Objective: To list factors that influence eye contact (gaze) during a dyadic conversation

> E. Nonverbal communication researchers believe there are many factors that determine the amount of eye contact (gaze) occurring during a conversation. After you observe conversations between people over the next few days, write a list of factors that affect eye contact (gaze) during a conversation between two people you observed.

UNIT 5
ENVIRONMENT

Can We Talk?

A. You are an executive in a large corporation. One day the president of the company calls you into his/her office and asks you to set up a meeting with other executives who are considered the decision makers of this organization. The purpose of the meeting is highly sensitive in that it calls for you to persuade your peers that the president's proposal (with which you secretly agree) is correct for the company. You know there are people against the president's proposal and that the president will not be at the meeting to lend his/her moral support. You have been given the choice of any room in the large complex to hold the meeting.

> What type of room would you choose that would help you to be the most influential? How would you arrange the furniture in the room? What kind of lighting would the room have? What color room would you choose? What other environmental factors would you consider?

B. In your opinion, how important are the concepts of proxemics/spatial relationships to the overall communication process? Take a position and support it with specific examples.

C. Have you found certain classrooms more conducive to learning than others? What are the environmental factors that make that classroom more conducive to you? Are any of those factors transferable to other places, for example restaurants, your home, etc.? Can you explain why these environmental factors are conducive to you?

D. Larry Keyes has been accused of picking the lock on the main entrance door to the dormitory. Technically he is guilty, but only of forgetting the key to open the front door entrance. Present at the hearing are Larry Keyes (the accused), a sophomore; Paul Super, resident advisor (junior); Betty Rooms, head resident advisor; Patrick

Liberal, a graduate student known for his radicalness; Peter Gotcha, head of dormitory maintenance (the accuser); and Dean Hohum, dean of students. Larry is aware of the fact that Super, Gotcha, and Hohum are ready to convict him and that Rooms and Liberal are generally sympathetic.

1. What suggestions would you make to Keyes regarding seating arrangements at the hearing?

2. What other advice would you offer Keyes in regard to the environment of the hearing room?

Actions Speak Louder Than Words

Objective: To help the student become aware of colors used in the environment

A. Break into small groups and canvass the campus buildings to determine what colors are used in various departments on campus.

> The president's suite?
> The admissions area?
> Research laboratories?
> Dining halls?
> Snack bars?
> Classrooms?
> Faculty offices?
> Student dormitories?
> Student center?

Note the colors used on walls, floors, furniture, and accessories. Compare notes in class.

Objective: To determine the effects environment has on learning

B. Hold the class meeting in different environments—an auditorium, a lounge, a restaurant, or outdoors, for example. Conduct the class as usual reserving fifteen to twenty minutes at the end of the class to discuss the problems or benefits apparent with the different learning environments.

Objective: To illustrate the importance of environment in a specific business

C. Imagine that you are a travel agent. Bring travel brochures/PowerPoint pictures to class as visual aids for a three-to-four-minute presentation to the class. You are to convince your classmates that "your agency" can offer them a dream vacation. Specifically describe the natural environment (terrain, vegetation, etc.), the hotel accommodations, entertainment establishments in the area, and other details of the vacation spot that you believe will appeal to your audience. At the conclusion of your presentation ask the class which of the visual aids illustrating the environment of the proposed vacation spot was most persuasive.

Objective: To gain insights from an expert on environments

D. Have an interior designer from campus or the community visit class with sketches and drawings illustrating the newest trends in office and home environments.

   Discuss your reactions to these trends.

Objective: To gain an understanding of music's contribution to environment.

E. Bring into class examples of various types of music. Prior to playing the recording suggest in what environment(s) this type of music might be beneficially/not beneficially utilized (for example in a hospital operating room, in a supermarket, etc.). A class discussion concerning the relationship of music and its impact on the perception of environment should follow.

On Your Own Time

Objective: To analyze the effect that space has on our perceptions

   A. As young children, most of us made tents out of old blankets or cloth over a clothes-line, stretched between two chairs, or over other sturdy objects. Why did we enjoy this activity?

      Spend at least one hour in a real or makeshift tent/a small room and write a short paper on how it feels to be in a confined space. Describe the setting, time of day, and comments by others who may have shared the experience with you.

Objective: To explore the relationship between the use of space and its effect on the activities that are conducted in that space

   B. Attend at least two events—for example a concert, reception, formal meeting, church service, or courtroom during a session. Compare and contrast the environmental settings associated with two or more events you choose to attend.

Objective: To use space creatively with a specific interior environmental goal

   C. Design the "perfect office" as defined by the office dimensions listed below. Working by yourself or in groups assigned by your instructor, choose one office design that demonstrates one of the following goals:

      1. an office that denotes status/control
      2. an office that denotes openness
      3. an office that denotes both status/control and openness

Dimension of the office and furnishings:
Office: 10 feet wide by 18 feet long
Desk: 3 feet wide by 5 feet long
3 filing cabinets: 1½ x 3 feet
1 table: 3 x 5 feet
4 chairs: 26 inches across each
1 couch: 3 x 6 feet
3 bookcases: 4 feet wide and 18 inches deep

Use graph paper at the end of this chapter for your floor plan.

What problems did you encounter?

How did you handle these problems?*

*Reference

Enid J. Portnoy, Virginia P. Richmond, *Nonverbal Communication Awareness*, (Morgantown, w. Va. The Book Exchange) p. 107. Copyright (c) undated. Reprinted by permission.

Objective: To stimulate awareness between spatial relationships and communication interactions

D. Below are diagrams of tables and chairs. Imagine that the situation is the school cafeteria and that each is the only table not occupied. For each of the eight diagrams, place an X where you and a friend of the same gender would seat yourselves for each of the four conditions noted.

1. Conversing, to talk for a few minutes before class

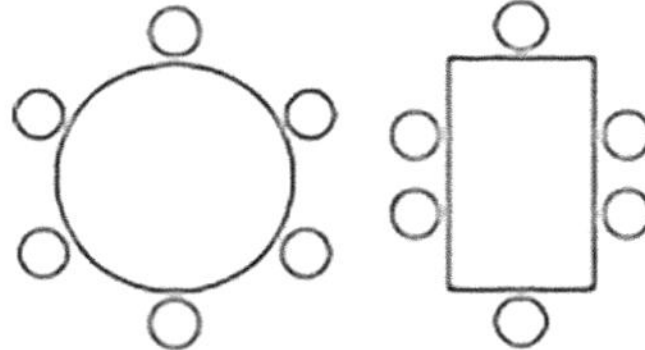

2. Cooperating to study together for the same exam or to work out a math problem

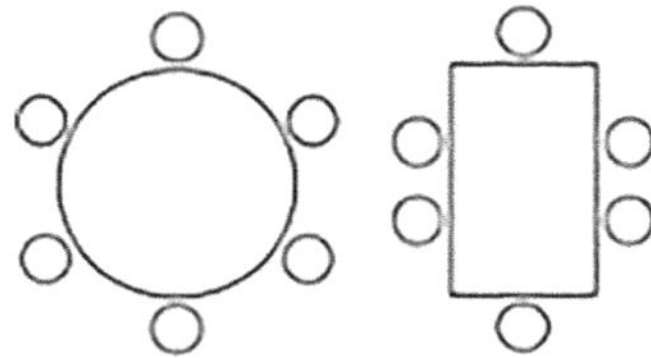

3. Co-acting to study for different exams

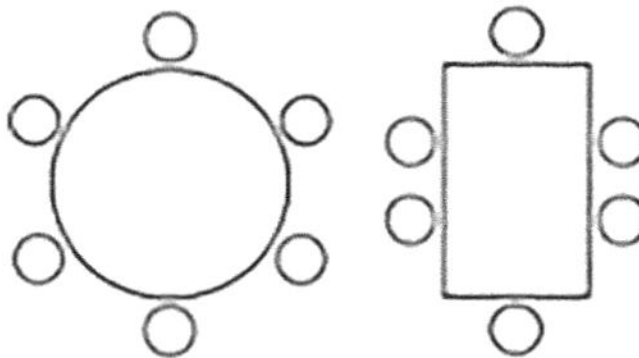

4. Competing against each other to see who would be the first to solve a series of puzzles

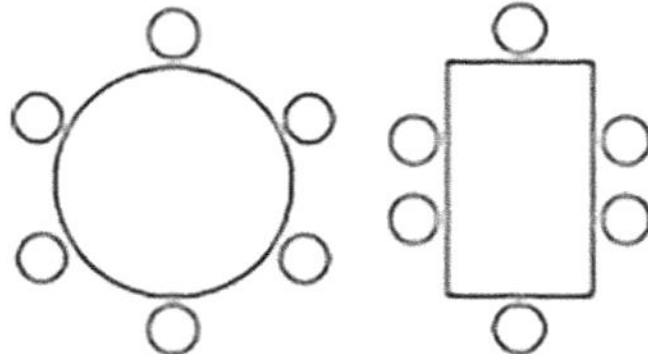

1. Why did you select the positions you did?

2. Explain the differences in opportunity for nonverbal interaction that the different positions allow.

3. How do these different positions relate to verbal communication?

4. Would you have chosen the same positions if the other person were of the opposite gender? Explain.

5. Compare your responses with the responses of others. How do you account for the differences in seating preferences?

6. Are there significant differences in choices between the round and the rectangular tables? Explain.*

Objective: To stimulate awareness between spatialrelationships and communication interactions

E. Below are presented diagrams of tables and chairs. Imagine that the situation is a cafeteria and this is the only table not occupied. In the space marked X is seated the person described abovethe diagram. Indicate by placing an X in the appropriate circle where you would sit.

1. A young man/woman to whom you are physically attracted and whom you would like to date but to whom you have never spoken

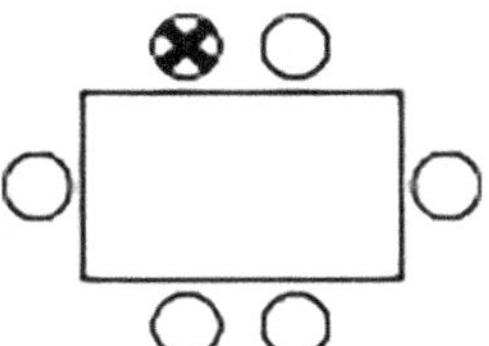

2. A person you find physically unattractive and to whom you have never spoken

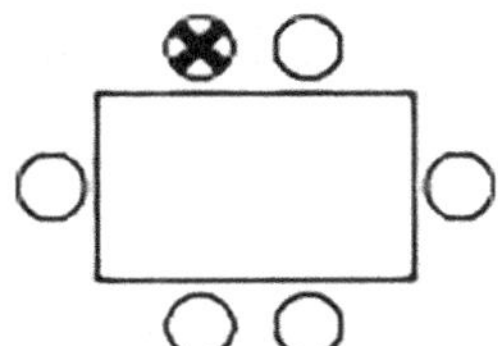

3. A person you dated once, had a miserable time with, and you would never date again

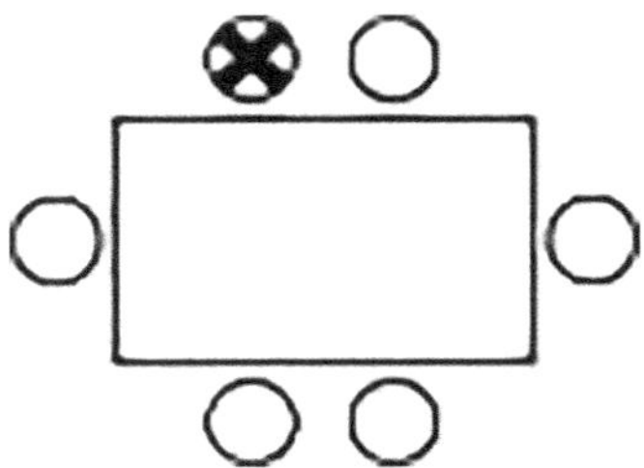

4. An instructor who gave you an F (which you did not deserve) in a course last semester and whom you dislike intensely

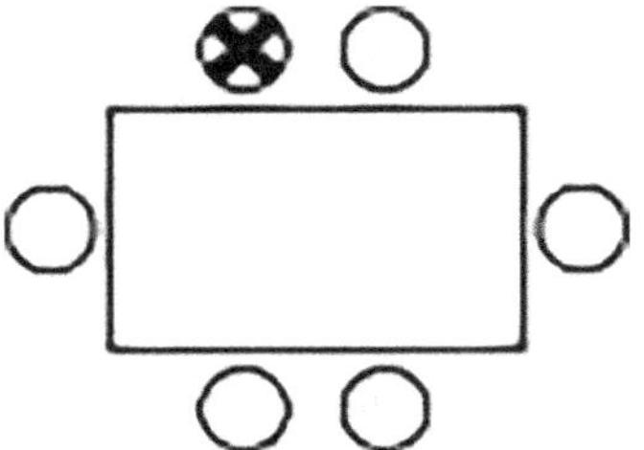

5. A person you have dated a few times and would like to date again

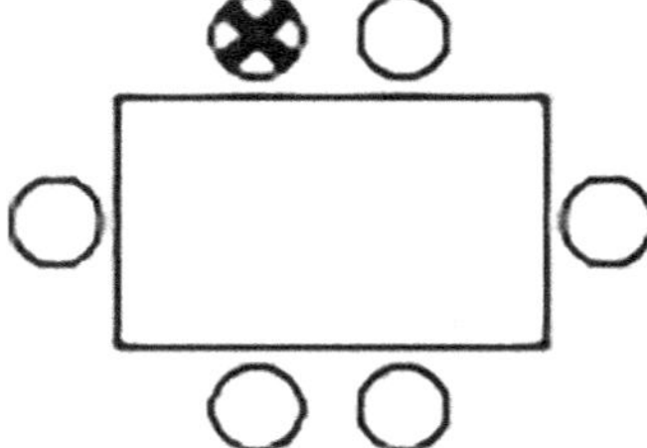

6. Your favorite instructor you would like to get to know better

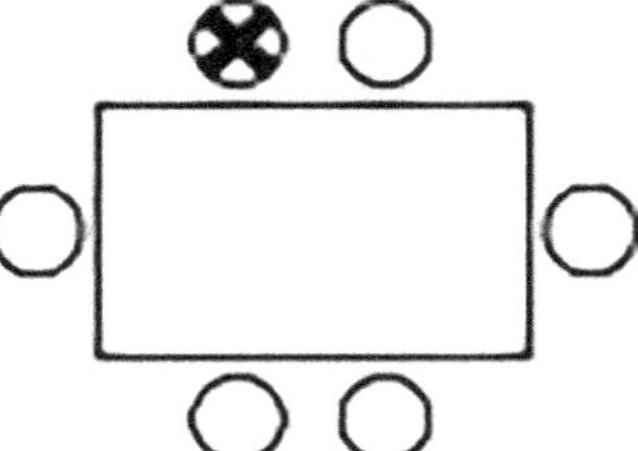

1. Why did you select the positions you did? For example, how does the position you selected enable you to achieve your purpose better?

2. Assume that you were already seated in the position marked X. Do you think that the person described would sit where you indicated you would (assuming the feelings and motives are generally the same)? Why? Are there significant sex differences? Significant status differences? Explain.

3. What does the position you selected communicate to the person already seated? In what ways might this nonverbal message be misinterpreted? How would
   your subsequent nonverbal (and perhaps verbal) behavior reinforce your intended
   message? That is, what would you do to ensure that the message you intend to
   communicate is in fact the message communicated and received?*

*Reference:

Robert Sommer, *Personal Space: Behavioral Basis of Design* (Englewood Cliffs 1 N.J.:
Prentice Hall) pp 61-73. Copyright (c) 1969. Reprinted by permission.

DESIGN THE PERFECT OFFICE

NAME: SCALE:

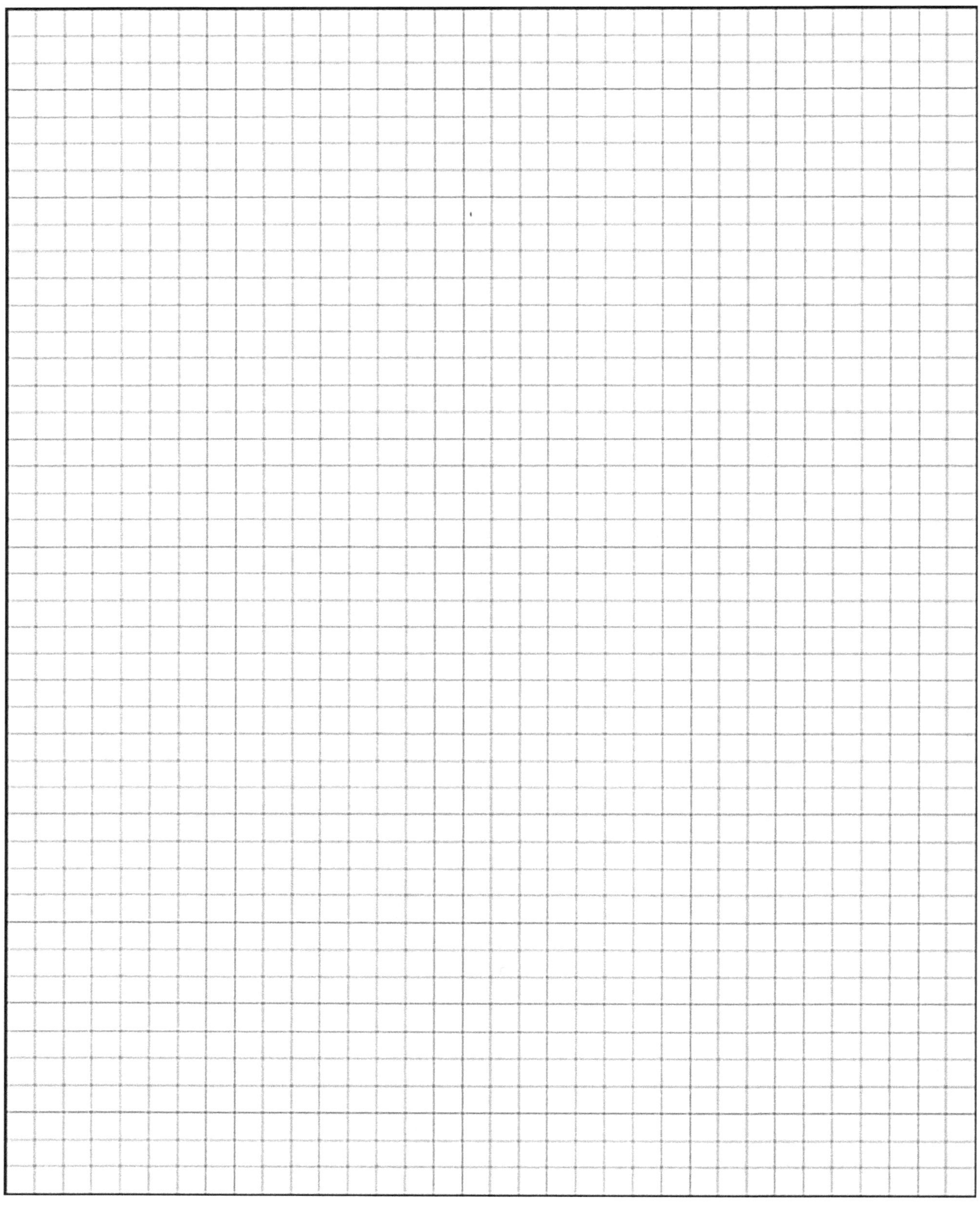

UNIT 6
PROXEMICS/PERSONAL SPACE; TERRITORY AND CROWDING

Can We Talk?

A. Anthropologist Edward T. Hall observed that there are four categories of informal space: intimate space, casual-personal space, social-consultative space, and public space. In what category would you place a situation such as the sharing of an armrest between two movie or theater seats? Are there other examples of situations such as during a viral pandemic that do not fit neatly into any of Hall's space categorizations?

B. List examples of using your body to prevent people from intruding on your private space. Share your examples with the class. Would these examples be altered during flu season or a viral pandemic?

C. There appears to be many factors that influence the use and perception of personal space. Discuss how you believe the following factors influence our use and perception of personal space. In addition include at least two additional factors you believe influence personal space.

     a. Culture
     b. Gender
     c. Topic/subject under discussion

In addition list at least two additional factors that might influence the use of personal space.

____

D. Give examples of contemporary and historical world events between nations of the world that involved disputes related to territory. On a more local level, are there any instances of conflict between different ethnic groups concerning space or territory? Finally, share with the class situations on this campus or in your living quarters where the use of space had to be discussed.

E. Based on your personal experiences, below write a brief narrative describing how territory/space had an impact on communication between you and another person.

Actions Speak Louder Than Words

Objective: To study the uses of personal space and crowding in a family setting

A. Each student should determine the number of people that sit at the family lunch/ dinner table. Draw a sketch of the table and the location of each person at the table (for example John usually sits here and Mary sits there). Depending on the number of people who sit at your family's dinner table, form small groups with students who have the same number of people sitting at their lunch/dinner table.

Discuss in your small group why the people who sit at your lunch/dinner table occupy those positions during the meal.

Which person appears to have the most room on the table? Who seems to be crowded?

Why is this?

How do you determine when your space on the table begins and end? Does the person who occupies the most room on the table also occupy the largest sleeping quarters in your home? Is this consistent with the person who occupies the least amount of space on the table?

What is the relationship between space on the table and age, gender, etc.?

Share your conclusions with your small group in the class.

Objective: To review the correlation between crowding and communication

B. List an experience on this campus where you were in a crowded space (for example cafeteria). How did the lack of space affect your verbal and nonverbal communication interaction with others?

Objective: To analyze the effects crowding has on listening and other behaviors

C. At the beginning of this lecture, students should place their desks close together (close enough that you could not easily stand up).

Prior to the conclusion of the lecture, students should discuss their perceptions of this seating condition.

Did the lack of space interfere with your ability to listen to the instructor's lecture?

Are there any other ramifications of having to sit in a close environment?

Objective: To think about territoriality

D. Each class member should sit in a different seat for one class meeting. Students should record their reactions to this new territory and share them with the class.

On Your Own Time

Objective: To observe cultural uses of space

A. Go to a fast-food restaurant prior to the lunch or dinner hour. Note the manner in which the patrons fill up the seats. Is there any pattern? Why are patterns formed? Were there any individuals who broke the pattern?

Why did they break the pattern? Did they hesitate to break the pattern?

Objective: To determine if gender affects space

B. Invite a group of three people to sit at a square table. The three people should not know each other well. Two of the people should be females and one a male. Note the pattern of sitting positions. Try this same experiment using different male-female combinations. What conclusions do you draw concerning the relationship between personal space and people's gender? Are there any factors other than gender that might explain seating position at a table?

Objective: To conduct a mini-experiment to study cultural uses of space

C. Each student should pair up with another student in the class. One student should be designated as a rule breaker while the other an observer. Each pair should decide on a mini-experiment whereby in an out of the classroom setting the student designated as the rule breaker enters into some situation where one or more rules of nonverbal communication are broken. The student designated as the observer should mentally note (to be written immediately following the situation) what occurred as a result of the rule breaking.

Some examples of mini-experiments that might be chosen are as follows:

Get on a bus with only a few people aboard and plenty of seats available. Sit next to one of the people aboard. This same mini-experiment can be performed in a cafeteria or office.

Get on an elevator with only one person aboard. Stand right next to that person rather than on the opposite side of the elevator.

Stand too close to a person while talking with the person.

NOTE: There are two rules that all mini-experiment participants must agree to.

First, the mini-experiment must involve some aspect of personal space, territory, and/or crowding.

Second, mini-experiment participants should not engage in any activity that will embarrass or endanger themselves or others significantly.

Report your findings to the class.

Objective: To analyze familiarity and its effect on space between people based on gender

D. Do people who are acquainted with each other as opposed to those not acquainted use space differently? Do two females differ in their use of space when they are acquainted/unacquainted with each other?

What about two males? Or a male and female? Observe in public places their non-verbal communication behavior. Be prepared to report your findings to the class.

UNIT 7
HAPTICS/TOUCH

Can We Talk?

A. As a very young child we explore much of our world through touch. As we grow older, we continue to learn about our world by using our sense of touch and also using other senses. Do you agree or disagree with this statement?

Take a position and support your views with examples in a class discussion.

B. Is there a relationship between touching and the nationality of a person? Does a relationship exist between touch and other variables, such as a person's gender, religion, financial status, or personality type? What other variables have an effect on touch?

C. What professionals are allowed to touch us in the course of their services to us? Why do we allow them to touch us? Are there any ethical codes that guide the touching behavior of professionals? Do any of these codes apply to parents? Have a class discussion.

D. Why do many researchers of nonverbal communication consider touch to be perhaps the most personal and essential of our senses? Do you believe that it plays an important part in human development from infancy to old age? During times of a seasonal flu or during a viral pandemic, how does the lack of touching one another impact our communication and general interaction with others? Give examples.

E. What was the religious act of "laying-on-of-hands" used for in the past? Why does it continue to be used by some healers to this day?

F. Although there are times when touch is accompanied by words, there are also times when touch is much more meaningful without words. Discuss occasions when touch need not be accompanied by words.

Actions Speak Louder Than Words

Objective: To establish the importance of touch based upon its frequent use in our language

A. In our language there are expressions that convey the importance of touch. As a class, add to the list below:

1. keep in touch
2. touch base with you
3.
4.
5.
6.
7.

Objective: To develop our appreciation for sense of touch

B. For this exercise, choose a class partner. Both partners (Person A and Person B) will agree to bring into the next class a small hidden (perhaps placed in a bag) three-dimensional object. During the next class, Person A should begin the exercise by closing his/her eyes. Person B will then hand his/her object to Person A, who should trace the configuration of Person B's object while simultaneously verbalizing a description of that object using only the sense of touch as she/he progresses in order to guess what the object is. Person B should make a note of Person A's description of the sensations he/she feels during this exercise. Reverse roles and start again. Discuss how the use of the sense of touch without the use of our other senses affects our perception of the world.

Objective: To become sensitive to tactile stimuli

C. Try to "get in touch" with the tactile stimuli around you. As a class call out the tactile stimuli that you are feeling while sitting in your desks. To put total concentration on this exercise, the class members should close their eyes. What have you discovered by doing this exercise?

Objective: To become aware of self-touch

D. How often do you unconsciously touch yourself (that is put your hands on your chin or ear)? During this class period, you should have another student seat himself/herself close to you in order to observe your touching behavior during the first half of the class. During the second half of the class, you should reverse roles. (A form for each student is provided on the next two pages to record you observations).

Observation Form

TOUCHING HAND TO:	FREQUENCY OF TOUCH
Hair	
Forehead	
Eyes	
Nose	
Ears	
Lips (moustache)	
Cheeks	
Mouth (Teeth/Tongue)	
Chin/Jaw (Beard)	
Neck	
Shoulders	
Upper Arm	
Lower Arm	
Wrists	
Hands (Fingers/Nails)	
Back	
Chest	
Stomach	
Buttocks/Genitals	
Upper Legs - above knees	
Knees	
Lower legs - below knees	
Ankles	
Feet (Toes)	

Observation Form

TOUCHING HAND TO:	FREQUENCY OF TOUCH
Hair	
Forehead	
Eyes	
Nose	
Ears	
Lips (moustache)	
Cheeks	
Mouth (Teeth/Tongue)	
Chin/Jaw (Beard)	
Neck	
Shoulders	
Upper Arm	
Lower Arm	
Wrists	
Hands (Fingers/Nails)	
Back	
Chest	
Stomach	
Buttocks/Genitals	
Upper Legs - above knees	
Knees	
Lower legs - below knees	
Ankles	
Feet (Toes)	

On Your Own Time

Objective: To study tactile behavior through a cultural and chronological perspective

    A. Visit a nursery school or kindergarten class for at least an hour. During your visit, observe the touching behavior between the male students, the female students, and the teacher. Did the male students touch the female students initially or did the female students initiate the touching behavior? Who initiated the touching between student and teacher? What conclusions did you reach concerning touching in these environments? Do these same touching behaviors exist in the college classroom? Why not? Share your findings with the class.

Objective: To research the correlation between tactile behavior and other variables

    B. During the course of your day (for example studying in the library, attending class, eating at a restaurant/cafeteria or with friends at a pub/bar) record all the socially acceptable forms of touching that you observe between people. What influenced the kind of touching? Share your findings with the class.

Objective: To establish how touching behavior is used with family/nonfamily individuals

    C. Among our family members we allow touching that would be inappropriate with a stranger. Think about the location and kind of touching behavior exhibited by your family members toward you. Does it vary? Why or why not? What other factors can you cite that influence touching behavior in your family? Compare your findings with others in your class.

Objective: To discover the uses of touch in various businesses

 D. Visit community businesses where touch is an important part of their activities, for examples garment factories, fruit and vegetable store, cosmetic stores. Write a short paper explaining tactile behavior in an industry. Share your findings with the class.

UNIT 8
VOCALICS/VOICE

Can We Talk?

A. As a class cite three famous people whose speaking voices are pleasing to you. Are there three people you consider as having a speaking voice that is irritating? What specifically are the vocal qualities that make a speaking voice pleasing or irritating to a listener?

B. Have you ever spoken to someone over the phone whom you have never met in person and yet have a mental picture of them? When you did meet them, did their physical characteristics match the image you had of them based upon their voice? Tell about an experience you had where you made certain assumptions about the way someone looked based solely on hearing their voice (for example a radio announcer). Specifically, what vocal qualities brought about the image of that person you created in your mind? Are there voice qualities in our culture that are associated with certain physical stereotypes? Give some examples (Hint: TV/movie animated productions).

C. Are certain vocal qualities (rate, pitch, volume) associated with specific professions (for example physician, automobile mechanic, etc.)? Discuss the various vocal qualities linked with occupations.

D. Describe the various dialects of English you have heard. How do they differ from the dialect that you speak? More specifically, does the rate, pitch, or volume, etc., differ from your dialect? Do dialects (for example British, Southern U.S., Boston) create images of that person? For fun, can you demonstrate for the class one dialect other than your own that you can speak? How did you learn to speak that dialect?

E. Can you tell whether people are lying by listening to their vocal qualities on a phone? Can you tell if they are unsure about something? How? Might these cues differ among people based on their geographical area, ethnic group, age group, etc.? Why are vocal qualities important during a courtroom trial?

Actions Speak Louder Than Words

Objective: To become more aware of your own voice

    A. Each student should select a partner in class and attempt to find their optimum pitch by using the following vocalic identification exercise:

        1. Hum a pitch that is comfortably low but not difficult to produce.

        2. Speak your name at that pitch - "My name is..."

        3. That pitch is "do," as in "do-re-mi-fa." Hum two pitches up from the "do" and speak at that pitch. "Mi" or "fa" should be what is called your *optimum pitch* or most natural pitch.

    After finding your optimum pitch, help your partner find his/her optimum pitch.*

Objective: To analyze the rate, pitch, and volume of various local dialects.

    B. Listen to three classmates' voices that have strong dialect traces. Listen to how the person uses the following words and spell them as the person pronounces them. Look for vocalic examples of northern, southern, and western dialects.

    Words:
    mother, father, coffee, stop, dog, time, cry, pin, still, interesting

    Ask three classmates to say: "My mother still drinks interesting coffee. My father's dog likes to cry. Pick up the pin."

    Describe and spell what you hear. **

Objective: To illustrate the importance of vocal variety in the communication process

C. Have two people read the following paragraph. The first person should read the paragraph without vocal imagery. The second person should read the paragraph with as much vocal imagery (varied pitch, rate, and/or volume, which allows the listener to visualize the images expressed in the paragraph) as possible.

> A cornfield in July is a sultry place. The soil is hot and dry, the wind comes across the lazily murmuring leaves laden with a warm, sickening smell drawn from the rapidly growing broad-flung banners of the corn. The sun, nearly vertical, drops a flood of dazzling light upon the field over which the cool shadows run, only to make the heat seem more intense.

Discuss the contrast between the first speaker's delivery compared to the second.
***

*Reference:

Enid J. Portnoy, Virginia P. Richmond, *Nonverbal Communication Awareness*, (Morgantown, W. Va.: The Book Exchange) p 77. Copyright (c) undated. Reprinted by permission.

**Reference:

Enid J. Portnoy, Virginia P. Richmond, *Nonverbal Communication Awareness*, (Morgantown, W. Va.: The Book Exchange) p. 76. Copyright (c) undated. Reprinted by permission.

***Reference:

Harrison M. Karr, *Developing Your Speaking Voice* (New York: Harper & Brothers Publishers) p. 290. Copyright (c) 1953. Reprinted by permission.

On Your Own Time

Objective: To show the communication relationship between gestures and voice

    A. What happens when gestures and voice are not compatible? Many actors have perfected humor based on incompatibility of voice with gestures. Are there any other actors who use incompatibility of voice and gestures to bring a humorous response from the viewer? Name a few movies/TV shows in which these incompatibilities are exhibited.

Objective: To explicate the various vocal styles used by professionals in different occupations

    B. Listen to recordings by politicians, comedians, clergy, and actors. Compare and contrast voice rate, pitch, and volume. What are the similarities and differences?

Objective: To gain insight into the work of professionals engaged in improving a client's voice quality

    C. For at least one-half hour observe online or in-person a voice professional (for example speech-language pathologist or public-speaking instructor) working with a client on improving a client's voice quality. What types of exercises does the professional use with the client?

Objective: To study how the human voice can bring about interest during a show or event

    D. What effect would the absence of cheering have on an athletic competition? What effect would the absence of an announcer have on athletic events?　Pick a sports event on TV. Describe the difference between viewing the TV sports event with sound and without sound.

Objective: To research the physical appearance—voice—stereotypes existing in our culture

E. Keeping the sound off on your TV, watch a cartoon show with which you are not familiar. If you had to give the cartoon character(s) voices, what rate, pitch, volume, and overall quality would you give them?   After determining the cartoon characters' voices, turn on the sound. Compare your voices with that of the cartoon characters and discuss the results with the class.

Objective: To examine cultural vocal stereotypes

F. Can you think of famous movie stars or TV personalities whose voices are considered (a) mild/harsh (b) weak/strong (c) low/high-pitched? What characters did they play in the movies or on TV? Why were they chosen to play those characters?

UNIT 9
CHRONEMICS/TIME

Can We Talk?

A. Describe an instance in which a misunderstanding concerning the correct meeting time resulted in one of the individuals being (a) ten minutes late (b) twenty minutes late (c) thirty minutes late. What kind of an effect did it have on the communication between the two individuals when they finally met?

B. Time, or chronemics, is culturally determined and defined. Do you agree or disagree with this statement? Give examples that illustrate your position.

C. Do individuals perceive time differently? What are some factors that affect the way people look at time (for example a person's occupation, retirement, etc.)?

D. What are the origins of our system of time in this country? How were the units of time determined (for example one hour equals sixty minutes, one day equals twenty-four hours, etc.)?

E. Do our bodies have "built-in clocks" that regulate our behavior and body functions? What are biorhythms? Do other forms of life on the earth exhibit behavior that is regulated by time? Give examples.

F. Give examples that reflect the use of terms or expressions that are time oriented in our language (for example I'll see you in a while, just a minute, etc.).

G. How do scientists who need very precise measurements of time record their data?

Actions Speak Louder Than Words

Objective: To measure one's skill in the perception of time

A. How accurate is your perception of time? The class should form groups of four. One person in each group should be designated the timekeeper (the timekeeper should use some form of timer). All group members should remain completely silent during this exercise. When the timekeeper announces "Start," try to estimate a one-minute time span. People should raise their hand when they believe one minute *exactly* has elapsed. The timekeeper should note the times that each participant signaled (for example fifty seconds, fifty-eight seconds, one minute and eight seconds). Which person was the closest to the one-minute mark? Repeat this exercise, except participants should close their eyes. Now, which person was closest to the minute mark? Were there any differences in the results between round one and round two? Why?

Objective: To determine our self-awareness of time

B. During this class lecture, place your timer on the desk for the first half of the lecture. Place your timer for the second half of the class in a place where it cannot be seen by you. Which half of the class lecture felt longer in time? Why? Why do you think that in places where there are large gambling casinos (for example Las Vegas) there are no clocks?

Objective: To study the relationship between time and light

C. At the beginning of this lecture the course instructor should lower the shades on the windows, blocking as much light as possible from the outside. If it is a night course, turn off one set of lights in the classroom. Ten minutes prior to the end of the class, a discussion should commence concerning whether this class felt longer or shorter than previous classes. Why is there a relationship between light and time perception? Does time seem to pass faster or slower when there are more daylight hours (for example summertime) as opposed to fewer daylight hours (for example wintertime)?

Objective: To make the student aware that he/she uses time when describing people

D. The concept of fast/slow time is ingrained in the way we perceive people. Examine the following list of people and decide which people you perceive as fast and which you perceive as slow:

urban/rural folks
people from hot/cold climates
heavy/thin people
educated/uneducated people

senior citizens/teenagers
happy/depressed people
military/civilian people
men/women

On Your Own Time

Objective: To consider the use of timing in entertainment

A. Go to a show which features comedians or watch a show on TV that has a comedian as a guest. As they deliver their monologue, note their timing. Is timing important to a comedian when telling a joke? What happens when children attempt to tell us jokes? What other types of entertainment uses timing?

Objective: To perform a self-analysis concerning the way we use time

B. How do you use your time? Time management is a method whereby you record the day's activities along with the amount of time devoted to each. By examining the day's record of activities, people are able to discover whether they use their time efficiently or not. Keep a diary for a day or two recording your hour-by-hour activities (this diary might be kept for an entire week). What times of the day were you most productive/least productive? Why? How can you use the time you waste more effectively?

Objective: To compare your "time" self-perception with others' "time" perception of you

C. Answer each of questions below. Next ask your close friends to rate you on the questions below without telling them your answers. Compare your "time" self-perception answers with your friend's "time" perception of you.

Scale: Relatively Slow(ly).... Relatively Quick(ly)

In most cases, I complete my school assignments ________________

In normal circumstances, I walk__________________.

In a calm situation, I am ______________________ to interrupt a speaker.

Compare your answers with your friends. Are they the same? If they are different, why?

Objective: To educate the student concerning the use of time in science

D. Examine the writings of Albert Einstein in an effort to understand his definition of time.

UNIT 10
GUSTATION—OLFACTORY/
TASTE AND SMELL

Can We Talk?

A. In a class discussion explore the relationship between taste and smell.

B. For many animals on the earth, the olfactory sense (sense of smell) is an important communication channel for mating. Some researchers agree that a large part of sexual attraction among human beings is based on the sense of smell. Do you agree or disagree? Are there any perfumes or colognes that advertisers claim will promote sexual attractiveness through the use of their product?

C. Describe instances where the exposure to certain scents elicited memories of a past experience or place.

D. Does taste sensitivity change with each ten years of life a person achieves (for example ten years of age, twenty, thirty, etc.)? Is it affected by the appearance of food? How does illness affect taste sensitivity and one's hunger urge? Take a position on these questions and defend your stance.

E. Is our taste for foods and drink something that we are born with, or does our environment dictate our likes and dislikes? Support your position in a class discussion.

F. Describe scent associated with different environments, for example a hospital, bakery shop, etc.

Actions Speak Louder Than Words

Objective: To test the student's olfactory ability

    A. Each student should bring to class a small brown paper bag containing an item (for example food, powder, etc.) that gives off a scent. Forming groups of three or four, number the bags, and then each person, without looking at the contents, should attempt to guess the item within each bag of the group (record each item as you sniff it). After each group member has had a chance to sniff each of the contents of the bags, group members should reveal the item. How many did you answer correctly? Did anyone in the group obtain all the correct answers? Which items did most of the group have difficulty identifying? Share your group results with the class in a class discussion.

Objective: To reveal to the student an expert's use of ingredients in preparation of foods

    B. Invite a gourmet chef into your class as a guest speaker. Ask her/him to speak about the various kinds of foods he/she prepares and the ingredients used to bring about the various tastes of each of the dishes.

Objective: To study the olfactory sensation in perfume/cologne

    C. Students should bring to class their favorite perfume or cologne. The student should mentally note the olfactory sensation he/she believes their perfume/cologne communicates to others through its fragrance. Forming groups of four or five, each person in the group should have a chance to smell the fragrance of the cologne/perfume of each of the other group member's perfume/cologne. Each person in the group should write down on a slip of paper the sensation conveyed through the fragrance (for example an ocean breeze, springtime etc.). Compare the group's responses to yours. Were there any surprises? Explain.

Objective: To explore the correlation between food color and smell/taste

D. Is there a relationship between the color of food and the way you expect it to smell
and taste? Bring to class foods that exhibit colors that reflect the flavor and smell
most people would expect it to have. Also bring to class foods (beverages are OK
too) that have colors that do not reflect the way most people would expect them to
be. Why are foods colored the way they are? Why do they smell the way they do?
Have a class discussion.

On Your Own Time

Objective: To study olfactory consistencies among people

    A. Using a sample of at least ten friends, ask what they consider to be the best smell. What is the worst scent? Was there a consistency among friends? Why or why not?

Objective: To seek information about the use of olfactory substances in religion

    B. Incense has traditionally been used in many religions around the world. Research online or visit clergy in your area and ask the purpose that incense plays in their religion. Are there other substances used in religious ceremonies that emit specific scents?

Objective: To conduct a taste test to determine our consistent likes and dislikes

    C. Go online or check out an international cookbook from your college or public library. Prepare and try to enjoy eating one ethnic dish contained in the cookbook. Later that week choose an ethnic restaurant that cooks the same dish you prepared earlier that week and order the same dish you made earlier that week. Did you like the dish you made or the restaurant's? How did the ingredients you used differ from that of the restaurant's? Are there some consistent ingredients used in different ethnic foods that you like or dislike?

Objective: To learn about other cultures' attitudes toward body odor

    D. Interview two international students from separate foreign countries. Ask them about their culture's general attitude about smell. Specifically ask about their country's use of lotions, cologne, deodorant, or powder to cover up body odor. Is bathing important in their country? If yes, how often do people bathe? What is their perception of our culture's use of products to cover up body odor?

SOME KEY TERMS
IN NONVERBAL COMMUNICATION

Key Terms Used in Nonverbal Communication

Can you define them?

Unit 1 - Introduction to Nonverbal Communication

chronemics ____

haptics ____

kinesics ____

oculesics ____

proxemics ____

vocalics ____

Additional terms your reading might include

____

____

____

____

Unit 2 - Physical Appearance and Dress

anorexia nervosa ______________________________________

cerebrotonic ____

ectomorph ____

endomorph ____

preening behaviors ____________________________________

somatotonic ____

viscerotonic ____

Additional terms your reading might include

____

____

____

____

Unit 3 - Kinesics/Body Movements and Gestures

adaptors ____

affect display ______________________________________

emblems ____

illustrators _______________________________________

regulators ____

Additional terms your reading might include

Unit 4 - Kinesics: The Face/Oculesics - Facial Expressions and Eye Behavior

affect blends _____________________________________

F.A.S.T. ____

C.L.E.M.S. ____

dilation and constriction ____________________________

Additional terms your reading might include

Unit 5 – Environment

dominance _______________________________________

status ____

macroenvironment/microenvironment ____________________

hi-load/low-load environment _________________________

Additional terms your reading might include

____

____

____

____

Unit 6 - Proxemics/Personal Space, Territory and Crowding

territoriality ____________________________________

violation _______________________________________

spot ____

k-space _______________________________________

markers _______________________________________

Additional terms your reading might include

____

____

____

____

Unit 7 - Haptics/Touch

deprivation ___________________________________

alienation _____________________________________

functional-professional touch ______________________

social-polite touch ______________________________

friendship-warmth-touch __________________________

Additional terms your reading might include

____

____

____

____

Unit 8 - Vocalics/Voice

vocal qualifiers _______________________________________

voice prints ____

dialect ____

time-compressed speech _______________________________

turn maintaining cues _________________________________

Additional terms your reading might include

____

____

____

____

Unit 9 - Chronemics/Time

monochronic/polychronic _______________________________

biorhythms ____

response latency _____________________________________

formal time ____

informal time _______________________________________

Additional terms your reading might include

____

____

____

____

Unit 10 - Gustation-Olfactory/Taste and Smell

smell blindness/adaptation _____________________________

smell memory ____

pheromone ____

taste blindness/adaptation _____________________________

food deprivation _____________________________________

Additional terms your reading might include

Suggested Research Projects

- Is interpersonal touch increasing or decreasing in this country as a result of technology?

- Is male-to-male touching changing? Why or why not?

- Is female-to-female touching changing? Why or why not?

- Is male-female touching behavior changing? Why or why not?

- How is touching behavior reflected in our dancing styles?

- What should the ideal male/female broadcast announcer's voice sound like?

- If modern technology permitted you to have any voice that you wished, what famous person's voice would you choose? Why? What kind of voice qualities did the people living fifty years ago consider ideal for a male and female radio/TV broadcaster?

- How do birthdays affect people's perceptions of themselves?

- Do all societies have a concept of time?   Why? Why not?

- What is the relationship between time and space?

- Is technology affecting the way we look at time?

- Is there a fourth dimension of time besides past, present, and future?

- What did the formal dress styles among men/women look like one hundred, five hundred, a thousand, and two thousand years ago?

- Study the dress of rock 'n' roll performers in the past. How did the dress of those performers reflect the times?

- Why do top executives choose the colors they do for formal work wear?

- Where did the use of men's ties and women's high heels come from?

- What are the functions of modern-day clothing?

- Trace the images of beauty through advertising since mass media started.

- How important is posture in public speaking at various functions?

- How would pantomime be used in a foreign country to express an idea?

- Trace the origins of some of our gestures.

- How will computer technology add to our gestures?

- Are there gestures that duplicate other gestures? Why?

- Why must we look at people when they are talking to us? What are the origins of this practice?

- Does the color of someone's eyes have an effect on persuasive behavior?

- What are the origins of our facial expressions? Why isn't a smile made like a frown?

- How is outer space exploration changing our perception of the earth's environment?

- Design office and living spaces fifty years from now/a hundred years from now.

- How will libraries be used in the future?

- How has the concepts of personal space, crowding, and national territorial boundaries been culturally altered since the COVID-19 pandemic? Are these cultural changes permanent?

- How is touch and listening related?

- How is touch employed in the average teaching environment, given viral pandemics?

ADDITIONAL SOURCES OF INFORMATION FOR NONVERBAL COMMUNICATION

The Basics of Nonverbal Communication: An Introduction

Argyle, M. *Bodily Communication*. New York: International Universities Press, 1990.

Bosmajian, J. (ed.) *The Rhetoric of Nonverbal Communication*. Ill.: Scott-Foresman, 1971.

Burgoon, J.K. and T. Saine. *The Unspoken Dialogue*. Boston: Houghton-Mifflin, 1978.

Davis, F. Inside Intuitions: *What We Know About Nonverbal Communication*. New York: McGraw-Hill, 1973.

DeVito, J.A. *The Elements of Public Speaking*. Harper & Row Publishers, Inc. 2013.

Fast, J. *Body Language*. New York: M. Evans, 1970.

Hall, E. T. *The Silent Language*. New York: Fawcett, 1959.

Harrison, R. *Beyond Words: An Introduction to Nonverbal Communication*. Englewood Cliffs, New Jersey: Prentice-Hall, 1974.

Knapp L. *Nonverbal Communication in Human Interaction*, 2nd Ed. New York: Holt, Rinehart and Winston, 2014.

Knapp, M. L. *Essentials of Nonverbal Communication*. New York: Holt, Rinehart and Winston, 1980.

LaRusso, D.A. *The Shadows of Communication*. Dubuque: Kendall/ Hunt, 1984.

Leathers, D. *Nonverbal Communication Systems*. Boston: Allyn & Bacon, 1976.

Malandro, L.A. and L. Barker. *Nonverbal Communication*. Reading, Mass.: Addison-Wesley, 1983.

Mehrabian, A. *Nonverbal Communication*. Chicago: Aldine, 1972.

Mehrabian, A. *Silent Messages*. Belmont: Calif.: Wadsworth, 1972.

Rosenfeld, L.B. and J.M. Civikly. *With Words Unspoken*. New York: Holt, Rinehart and Winston, 1976.

Ruesch, J. and W. Kees. *Nonverbal Communication: Notes on the Visual Perception of Human Relations*. University of Southern California Press, 1956.

Weitz, S. (ed.) *Nonverbal Communication Readings with Commentary*. New York: Oxford University Press, 1974.

Zunin, L. *Contact: The First Four Minutes*. New York: Ballantine Books, 1986

Physical Appearance and Dress

Berscheid, E. and E.H. Walster. *Interpersonal Attraction.* Reading, Mass.: Addison-Wesley, 1969.

Molloy, J.T. *Dress For Success.* New York: Warner Books, 1988, and *Woman's Dress for Success Book,* Chicago: Follett, 1977.

Rudofsky, B. *The Unfashionable Human Body.* Garden City, N.Y.: Doubleday & Co., 1971.

Sheldon, W.H. *Atlas of Man: A Guide for Somatypinq the Adult Male at All Ages.* New York: Harper & Row, 1954.

Kinesics/Body Movements and Gestures

Davis, F. *Inside Intuition.* New York: McGraw-Hill, 1973.

Efron, D. *Gesture, Race and Culture.* The Hague: Mouton, 1972.

Hanley, N. *Body Politics: Power, Sex and Nonverbal Communication.* Englewood Cliffs, N.J.: Prentice-Hall, 1977.

Laban, R. and L. Ullman. *The Mastery of Movement.* Amazon.com: Boston,1971

Morris, D. *Manwatching: A Field Guide to Human Behavior.* New York: Harry N. Abrams, 1979.

Scheflen, A.E. and A. Scheflen, *Body Language and the Social Order.* Englewood Cliffs, N.J.: Prentice-Hall, 1972.

Kinesics: The Face/Oculesics - Facial Expressions and Eye Behavior

Argyle M. and M. Cook, *Gaze and Mutual Gaze.* Cambridge: Cambridge University Press, 1976.

Ekman, P. and W.V. Friesen. *Emotion in the Human Face.* Elmsford, N.Y.: Pergamon Press, 1972; and *Unmasking the Face.* Englewood Cliffs, N.J.: Prentice-Hall, 1975.

Ekman, P. (ed.). *Darwin and Facial Expression.* New York: Academic Press, 1973.

Ekman, P. "Facial Signs: Facts, Fantasies, and Possibilities," in T. Sebeok (ed.). *Sight, Sound and Sense.* Bloomington, Ind.: Indiana University Press, 1978 1 pp. 124-156.

Hess, E.H. *The Tell-Tale Eye.* New York: Van Nostrand Reinhold, 1975.

Lafrance, M. and C. Mayo. *Moving Bodies: Nonverbal Communication in Social Relationships.* Monterey: Brooks/Cole, 1978.

Worthy, M. *Eye Color, Sex and Race.* Anderson, S.C.: Drake House/ Hallux, 1974.

Environment

Hall, E.T. *The Hidden Dimension.* Garden City, N.Y. Doubleday, 1966.

Knapp, M.L. *Nonverbal Communication in Human Interaction,* 8th Edition. New York: Holt, Rinehart and Winston, 2013.

Leather D.G. *Nonverbal Communication Systems.* Boston: Allyn Bacon, 1976.

Mehrabian, A. *Public Places and Private Places.* New York: Basic Books, 1976.

Newman, O. *Defensible Space.* New York: Macmillan Publishing Co., 1972.

Sommer, R. *Personal Space: The Behavioral Basis of Design.* Englewood Cliffs, N.J.: Prentice-Hall, 1969.

Proxemics/Personal Space, Territory, and Crowding

Altman, I. *The Environment and Social Behavior. Belmont, Calif. Wadsworth, 1975.*

Ardrey, R. *The Territorial Imperative:* New York: Antheneum 1966, 2014.

Freedman, J. L. *Crowding and Behavior.* New York: Viking Press, 1975.

Goffman, E. *Behavior in Public Places: Notes on the Social Organization of Gatherings.* New York: The Free Press, 1963.

Hall, E. *The Silent Language.* New York: Anchor Press, 1973.

Sommer, R. *Personal Space: The Behavioral Basis of Design.* Englewood Cliffs, N.J.: PrenticeHall, 1969.

Haptics/Touch

Henley, N.M. *Body Politics: Power, Sex and Nonverbal Communication.* Englewood Cliffs, N.J.: Prentice-Hall, 1977.

Howard, J. *Please Touch: A Guided Tour of the Human Potential Movement.* New York: McGraw-Hill, 1970.

Montagu, M.F.A. *Touching: The Human Significance of the Skin*. New York: Columbia University Press, 1971.

Morris, D. *Intimate Behaviour*. New York: Random House, 1971.

Vocalics/Voice

Guiles, H. and P.F. Powesland. *Speech Style and Social Evaluation*. New York: Academic Press, 1975.

Fairbanks, G. *Practical Voice Practice*. New York: Harper and Brothers, 1944.

Ostwald, P.F. *Soundmaking*. Springfield, Ill.: Charles C. Thomas, 1963.

Chronemics/Time

Hall, E. *The Hidden Dimension*. New York: Doubleday Publishing Company, 1966.

Kubler, G. *The Shape of Time*. New Haven: Yale University Press, 1962.

Luce, G.G. *Body Time; physiological rhythms and social stress*. New York: Holt, Rinehart & Winston, 1971.

Gustation-Olfactory/Taste and Smell

Hall, E. *The Hidden Dimension*. New York: Doubleday Publishing Company, 1974.

Thomas L. *The Lives of a Cell*. New York: Doubleday Publishing Company, 1974 (London, England: Penguin Publishing Company, 1978).

Additional information on nonverbal communication may be found in the following publications:

Journals

Abnormal Psychology
Applied Behavioral Science
Applied Psychology
Applied Social Psychology
Canadian Journal of Behavioral Science
Central States Speech Journal
Comparative Psychology
Communication Monographs
Communication Quarterly
Journal of Consulting and Clinical Psychology
Journal of Developmental and Educational Psychology
Environmental Behavior
Experimental Child Psychology
Genetic Psychology Monographs
Human Communication Research
Human Relations
Journal of Communications
Personality and Social Psychology
Psychology Today
Psycholinguistic Research
Psychosomatic Medicine
Quarterly Journal of Speech
Review of Educational Research
Speech and Hearing Research

Books of Interest

Bowden, M. *Winning Body Language: Control the Conversation, Command Attention, and Convey the Right Message without Saying a Word.*

Driver, J. *You Say More Than Think: A 7 Day Plan for Using Body Language.*

Ekman, P. *Emotions Revealed, Second Edition.*

Goman, C.K. *Silent Language of Leaders: How Body Language Can Help or Hurt How You Lead.*

Houston, P. Floyd, M. Carnicero, S . Tennant, D *Spy the Lie: Former CIA Officers Teach You How to Detect Deception.*

Navarro, J. *The Dictionary of Body Language.*

Navarro, J. Karlins, M. *What Every Body is Saying: A Ex-FBI Agent's Guide to Speeding-Reading People.*

Pease, A. Pease, B. *The Definitive Book on Body Language: The Hidden Meaning Behind People's Gestures and Expressions.*

Reiman, T. *The Power of Body Language: How to Succeed in Every Business and Social Encounter.*

Segle, H. *Body Language: Discover and Understand the Psychological Secrets Behind Reading and Benefitting from Body Language.*

Turchet, P. *The Secrets of Body Language.*

Wendler, D. *Improve Your Social Skills.*

Wezowski, K. Wezowski, P. *Without Saying a Word: Master the Science of Body Language and Maximize Your Success.*

NOTES

NOTES

NOTES